SHINE

Ufomadu Consulting & Publishing Group

SHINE

Ufomadu Consulting & Publishing Group

Dr. Udo F. Ufomadu

© 2021 by Ufomadu Consulting & Publishing. All rights reserved.

No part of this publication may be produced without prior permission of the copyright holder, except as provided by USA copyright law.

ISBN 978-1-7331255-2-9

Part 1

THE DEVIL IS OBSESSED WITH YOU BECAUSE YOU MATTER; IGNORE HIM AND FOCUS ON MATTERS THAT MATTER.

We have to learn how to ignore distractions that are orchestrated by the negative forces and the devil in particular. When they realize that we are on the right track, and consistently doing things that we are supposed to do without letting them stop us, they flee. To resist the devil does not necessarily imply that you should engage in a physical fight or verbal abuse; however, a constructive verbal response may be needed. Evaluate this constructive verbal responses from Jesus. The devil says, "If you are the son of God tell these stones to become bread." Jesus answered, "It is written man shall not live by bread alone but by every word that comes from God's mouth." The devil told Jesus to jump from a very highpoint and that God will send His angels to protect him. Jesus answered, "Do not put the Lord your God to test." Again, the devil showed Jesus all the kingdoms of the world and their splendor and promised to give it to Jesus if he bows down and worship him. Jesus firmly responded, "Away from me Satan, for it is written, worship the Lord your God and serve him only." Then, the devil left Jesus and the angel came and attended to Jesus. It is not necessarily what is done or said to you that matters in the end, it is how you react to it. If you react constructively, your haters will flee, and angels will subsequently attend to you. We all experience challenges or difficult times, which I do not believe come from God, that God utilizes to make us stronger and better people.

Arise and shine with no regrets because everything that you touch these days, turn to gold. Your gifts have continually opened doors that lead to greatness. Continue to be focused on things that are meaningfully enriching to you, your family, friends, community, and God. When your focus is on doing good, it shows, and God rewards you. When you shine accordingly, others will notice it and glorify our God. The more our God is glorified for the good things that you do, the more you are rewarded.

God has so many good things for us to do and have, but we have to be willing to internalize the fact that we matter. Certainly, we all have promises that God firmly put in our hearts. He gave us a dream to stand on. He is the one who instilled that hope in us by assuring us that problems will definitely turn around. He is the one who called us blessed, treasure, healed, productive, overcomer, and forgiven. Furthermore, he wants us to obey him; He wants us to ignore distractions that tamper with our importance. Some of these distractions can weigh you down and, at times, result to depression as the devil plans. The truth of the matter is that, when you are depressed, it is harder to willingly and continually do great things because you no longer hear from God like you should. Be happy, for sadness steals your productive references but the joy of the Lord strengthens you, so be happy each day for each day is another blessed day. Steer away from unnecessary competition. Pray more and worry less about issues. Be grateful, be contented, pursue peace, believe that tomorrow will be better, appreciate other people's gifts and talents, never claim to be all knowing, and walk in love all the time. As a matter of certainty, the quickest way to be happy is by making somebody happy. What you make happen for others, God makes happen for you. When we talk about happiness, money readily comes to mind but amazingly there are things money cannot buy. Do not expect happiness to be that special package that someone else will put together for you; it is a package that you'll put together for yourself.

Sometimes those that go out of their way to help others are, at times, ridiculed and called names that are derogatory, pejorative, or just make it appear as if they are unwise. But amazingly, they are the wise ones; those who realized that the more you help others, the more God helps you. In order to totally harness the importance that God installed in you, one must, to an extent, shake off selfishness and self-centeredness just like a tree would shake off dead leaves and grow new leaves of unselfishness or selflessness.

It pays to be yourself and not live like everybody wants you to live. Remember, you are not programmed to conform to everybody's plan because God specifically programmed you to be peculiar with your own gifts and talents; not someone else gifts and talents. We are all fully loaded with gifts and talents, but most people do not focus on their gifts and share from them, rather, they focus on somebody else's gift and the lies that the devil tells. Invest more time and energy on what you'll give from your gift or talent, not what you'll get from others, and you will be amazed at your return on investment (ROI).

No matter how gifted or talented you are, try not to be perceived as very prideful or as a person who always flaunts his or her talent at the expense of group, community, or organizational goals and objectives. We must respect those that God put ahead of us, but you must also realize that your victory or success is never dependent upon what another person does or says but totally on what God says or does. Be guided and guarded, for your gift or talent can also arouse envy to the point that people you trust and people that are supposed to look out for you can connive to hurt you, but always remember that the God that you have continued to serve will utilize such plots as routes to your superstardom. Even if you discover their plot, remain focused on God and continue to be your good self and leave the battle to our omnipotent God. This is not the time to prove that you are a problem solver or analytical maestro. It is the time to be humble and totally dependent on God. You'll have to focus undistractedly on our problem solver than on the problem itself, because our problem solver is bigger than any plan or plot. Consequently, you have minimized the problem by magnifying our God. At this point, you must realize that a garment of sadness cannot fit you, but a garment of praise will fit you perfectly, so put on the garment of praise. Prioritize feeling good, smiling, and laughing as needed. Afterall, laughter or smiling does not undermine you in any way, rather it is depression that undermines your health and personality.

While the coup plotters get judged in God's on way for harming the one that has not done any wrong, the good one whose steps are directed by God will eventually and usually receive God's favor beyond imagination. Even after God's favor has landed you some meaningful acquisitions or promotions, you must continue to be good and never allow the new things that God is doing in your life to affect how you treat others. Continue to be that person who rejoices, also, when others experience success, victory, or other blessings. Continue to be that one who loves to give. Continue to be that person who utilizes his or her capacity to bring peace among warring factions.

Continue to believe that the only reason that the devil is obsessed with you is because you matter. Grin, joke, be positive, ignore the devil and remain focused for our God always has something worthy to say. God talks to us in many ways, so a lack of focus, anger, or depression will distract and divert your attention wrongly. God talks to us through life experiences. God speaks to us internally. God utilizes bible verses to speak to us. God uses other people to speak to us, such as anointed reverends, pastors, apostles, bishops etc. In consideration of the preceding, a distracted person can easily minimize his or her importance by not hearing from God and constantly disrespecting himself / herself, or others and relating poorly to people around him. When you are focused, your title, wealth, and other acquisitions do not affect how you treat others. Vengeance is handed over to God. You treat every body with respect regardless of what differentiates you from them. If we ignore distractions, we can abide easily by this biblical advice that is accepted in every culture of the world, "do not rebuke an older man but encourage him as you would your father, younger men as your brother, older women as your mothers, and younger women as sisters in all purity."

We matter. We definitely matter, for we are created in God's image. We matter because the all-knowing, all powerful, and ever present God cares about our needs. We matter, and that's why God sent his son to die for our sins. We are important, and that is why our past mistakes cannot stop us from maximizing our potential. That is why our importance is further established when we use our gifts to make God happy and ourselves happy too. Singular success may be inadequate in this case; you want to utilize your gift in making this world a better place to live. Yes, I want you to succeed because your success is our success.

Part 2

I WANT YOU TO SUCCEED BECAUSE YOUR SUCCESS IS OUR SUCCESS.

Five people in a group with a total income of $300,000 may be more beneficial to their group and community than one person making $500,000 while the other four do not have meaningful income. This becomes substantiated when you consider the fact that each member of the group has needs, like food and shelter. Moreover, they are likely to have churches, banks, retail outlets, grocery stores, and natural and spiritual families that need their support in the community. Remember, they pay taxes that benefit the community and children's education. Regardless of how the individual that makes $500,000 tries to extend support, it will never be sufficient. My point here, is that group success is far more relevant than personal success. Everybody should put their gifts to work and open up businesses. Be humble and find work; even if it is not exactly what you want, keep giving it your best and what you want will show up. If you become a good steward with little, God will give you more. Regardless of how much your make, know ye that your shopping, your taxes, your support for businesses and services like banks, barbershops, car repair shops, hair salon, support for churches, support for schools, your house/apartment related bills and rents and etc. help to make a community a better place to live.

The best way to get group effectiveness is through respect for all. A team that wants all in the team to succeed must value each other. The team must recognize that each person in the team is capable of being successful. We all have our unique gifts, strengths, and weaknesses. Unique gifts and strengths must be encouraged to flourish, while weaknesses should be handed to God with the hope that, He will transform it to strength when He wants.

If you are in a group and someone is doing better than you, envy and unwarranted aggression will not solve your problem. Rather, you need to wait for your own time because God is no respecter of people. Continue to be a happy person, because happy inputs translate to happy outputs. Don't make the mistake of waiting until your situation changes before experiencing the joy of the Lord. The joy of the Lord is our strength, and we constantly need that capacity in order to experience the ongoing life of victory that God has in store for us. Instead of resorting to envy and bullying, find out what the person who has already got what you are looking for chooses to glorify, adore, worship, and some of his or her regular practices. Successful people set clear practices and goals. They comprehend that there is power in giving and they choose to maintain a relationship with a force that is all knowing, a force that is all powerful, and a force that is everywhere. This force as far as I am concerned is no respecter of persons. He does not discriminate. What He does for Mr. A or Mrs. A is available to Mr. B or Mrs. B, as long as they are willing and obedient.

Furthermore, successful people respect and love others. They know that respect is a necessary ingredient for personal and overall growth. They also know that team members usually bring their best when they feel respected and empowered. It pays, in group or community settings, when everybody is empowered to succeed so that they can contribute their fair share and have sense of belonging and care about the group, organization, or community.

The love and respect that successful people allow to reign in their midst minimizes conflict. Conflict, when handled improperly, can degrade any group. Disagreements are unavoidable in a successful group and may even help members to be meaningfully analytical. Great groups, based on my experience and learning, respect each other and work through disagreements, instead of allowing disagreements to split them. Disagreements, if effectively managed, can be a source that lifts the group.

Team members tend to give their best when they feel that they are loved and recognized. Also, team members give their best if they know that they are valued and will benefit directly from the team. In order to be successful as a group, it is essential to have a mutual respect for each other, have common goals, have open communication, and have good benefits.

The main reason that most companies pay well and come up with some benefits is to be able to compete for good employees. Once a company has benefits like retirement program, group insurance, profit sharing, and etc. such company is considered by most good employees, in that community, as a good company. Such benefits draw good workers who, in turn, help the company to remain competitive and profitable.

Some organizations give their employees the opportunity to pursue further education with increased pay and status. These organizations establish tuition refund programs and will, at times, arrange with community colleges and universities to educate their employees. Whether as an employee, employer, or other team member, it is great to remain a good team member.

A good team member does not criticize everything and everybody; a good team member covers the mistake of a fellow team member while the game is going on, but talks about it later; a good team member is not all knowing, a good team member is dutiful; a good team member is empathetic; a good team member is humble; and a good team member will apologize to you if he or she offends you; and a good team member puts the interest of the team first before his or her interest.

As you continue to be that humble, Godfearing, and empathetic team member, God will continue to crown you with victory. Remain grateful to God, keep your head up and celebrate your victories and also celebrate the fact that you are a treasure to behold. Check this reality out: you are God fearing, a team player, an asset to God's kingdom, creative, peace-loving, humble, empathetic, a visionary, respectful, a prophet, enterprising, prayerful, and resourceful; no wonder the devil is obsessed and mad at you.

Continue to amalgamate your God-given gifts with hope and trust in the Lord and the outcome will continue to be outright consequential in group settings and personal transactions. If loving peace and fearing God in team situations makes the devil mad, then make him mad. Let me tell you this: when peace shrinks in a place, money consequently shrinks too. Make sure that team resources are used well. It is not even about how much resources a team or group has, it is about the optimum utilization of the resources.

Support your team whenever your team supports education. When we wisely invest in education, we get gargantuan return on investment by making ourselves better, by attracting industries that are subsequently attracted by our enlightened work force, by having an increased tax base, and by investing our rich tax money to make our community loveable.

We must strive for improvement regardless of the setting. We must improve any ammunition that is designed to fight division in our group. Division and unwarranted criticism are proven sources of instability in a community or group. Your personal life and your group's life will definitely become fulfilling when you begin to see less of weaknesses and focus more on strengths and the good in the people around you.

Do not be too knowledgeable to involve God in your group's dealings. If allowed by law, acknowledge God openly before your sessions begin and He will direct the meeting. Because you have genuinely and respectfully involved God in the things that you do, it is no wonder that wisdom has saturated your decision making.

When you first show up in a group, those who do not know you well may form wrong opinions of you. Do not let their wrong opinions stick. Never become satisfied with people's improper definition of you. Be consistent in well doing, support what is right and not who is right; respect and love all and continue to pray for those who do not know that the devil is using them to destabilize your group's excellent intentions. Our God answers prayers, and He will eventually turn things around when He deems fit, and your group will shine and cause good and great concerns.

Your packaging is critical from your first time with the group to your last time. You must package yourself as a lover of improvement, as an overcomer, as a peace lover, and as a child of God.

Though people in a team may come from different backgrounds, a true team is not formed until unity becomes essential to everybody on the team and until winning, also, becomes everybody's goal. If self-centeredness and selfishness take center stage to the point that unity is disregarded, the outcome is usually retrogressive.

For great outcomes to manifest in your team, group, or community, you must steer away from hostility, baseless pride, hate, and politics of bitterness because these factors lead to disrespect and lack of love which, in turn, negatively affect the team's posture. Yes, you matter. This is the reason the devil is upset with you. Continue to ignore the devil; I'm praying that you will continue to shine for I am one hundred percent certain that your success is our success.

Part Three

SHINE QUOTES

Utterly scorn the devil's misrepresentations but think well of yourself, your achievements, your sacrifices, and your blessings.

Sadness will infringe on your ability to shine effectively because it steals your productive preferences, but the joy of the Lord strengthens you, so be very happy for today is another blessed day.

The quickest way to be happy and shine in a manner that causes concern for the devil, is to make someone else happy even when you have your own challenges.

Let us laugh more and shine this day; after all, laughter or smile does not undermine us, but uptightness does.

Don't look down, rather look up for your sustainable victory is not dependent upon what people do or say but upon what God says and does.

Lord help me shine my little light as I desire to be a blessing and put smile on faces, not just with money, but in other ways too.

I love the fact that other people's success/victory/ blessings make you smile and rejoice.

Keep shinning and flying as the eagle for no devil, witch, or diabolic has the capacity to stop you.

I know what God's providence decrees and I am convinced that every potential in you will be maximized.

Hold your head high and keep shinning for adversity does not translate to God's anger upon thee.

Shine even when adversity stares you in the face, for in the absence of temporary adversity, one may easily slack in praying to that force whose names are holy, our help, rock, Mighty In Battle (MIB), Pa-Chineke, Jehovah, all knowing, all-powerful, and ever-present.

Remain positive even when negativity encompass you.

Exclude self-pity today and include God's promises like "I will not leave you nor forsake you." "I will give you beauty for ashes." "I will help you." "I will uphold you."

Shine with alacrity for God is your strength and hope like no other.

Continue to gallantly reject those garments of discouragement, depression, and despondency that fit you never.

Be grateful and keep your little light shining for God is pleased with you.

BELIEVE that God called you an overcomer; RECEIVE that you will be mightily blessed this month as you bless others too.

Smile in anticipation because your miracle is very nigh.

Your enemies, including lack, haters, and sickness are running to a point of no return for God confused and dispersed them; be happy and keep shinning.

Continue to be good and never lose your enthusiasm; after all, all things work together for your good.

You'll keep shinning as long as you undistractedly focus on God, your problem solver and not on the problem for our problem solver is bigger than any problem.

If being empathetic, shining, peace-loving, respectful, prayerful, nice, kind, resourceful, and an asset to God's kingdom make the devil mad, then make him mad.

Young and old are gravitating toward your light, so keep shinning for the Lord is in your corner.

Disregard darkness and keep appreciating and developing yourself, plus others, positively with God's support and splendor for your light has come; and God's glory is obviously risen upon you.

Shine for it's what God calls you that matters; He calls you blessed, treasure, healed, productive, overcomer and forgiven.

Get up, shine for evil forces bow at the call of your God's name.

Refuse to wear garments of bitterness because it negatively alters your radiance.

Shine and I say shine for nothing can stand against Jesus.

The more you alleviate others' problems, the more God alleviates your problem.

Keep shinning and never allow the devil's tactics to dry you up because you cannot deliver spiritually and materially if you don't have anything.

The more you utilize your influence the way that pleases God, the more influential thou shall become.

Regardless of circumstances, you must not fail to shine by operating in love 'cause love is enduring, kind, and never fails.

Continue to be part of the solution, not part of the problem.

Keep your head up and shine in a manner that will cause great concern for the devil and his operatives.

If your smile bothers the devil, keep shining, keep smiling for the Lord your strength, covers every weakness.

Remain happy and positive, not because things are perfect, but because your God is bigger than any issue.

Smile, for you are an asset and a treasure to behold.

Always magnify the Lord who causes you to shine, don't magnify issues.

Continue to radiate and realize that negative things are sometimes thrown from known and unknown; regardless, thou shall never claim to be their victim.

Remain humble, hopeful, and prayerful; God is about to crown you with another victory.

Though the storm rages, thy boat will never sink because Jesus is in thy boat.

How the devil sees your light matters not, all we know is that the glory of God is risen upon you.

Be happy for you've boarded Jesus' victory train which glides smoothly into the extra ordinary stations of strength, wisdom, and love.

You have remained blessed in spite of these distractions because your hope and trust are rigidly in the Lord.

Smile radiantly because your way maker has transformed those blocking you to those backing you.

Continue to be a valuable team member in the pursuit of total victory over evil.

You are a good person, so allow God, not your critics, to keep directing your steps.

Focus on what God vindicates; not on what the devil fabricates.

Stay strong, keep walking in love; God and those who know you well will always refute wrong assumptions made about you.

Shine, for your God is far greater than these distractions.

Feel successful, not because all is great yet but because God is so pleased with you.

You'll continue to rise higher until you maximize the potential God installed in you.

The more you count your blessings, the more you elevate your positive attitude.

Continue to be your group's advocate for peace, love, and unity; no role is more significant.

Shine by remaining peaceable, empathetic, and respectful; for these are the traits of the wise.

What your enemies have not realized yet is that every time they talk or plan against you, it moves God's action in your favor.

Your light can never be quenched by humans.

The more you embrace unity, the more you bother the enemies of progress.

You've always blessed, prayed for, and just helped others in the midst of your storm because you realize it is very rewarding.

Continue to shine and never allow your past disappointments to consume your enthusiasm.

Continue to choose wisely; choose groups that forbids unnecessary internal quarrels.

Any group that avoids unnecessary fights, avoids unnecessary fall.

Classy people remove the logs in their eyes before talking about specks in another person's eyes.

Remain good to the point that negativity will hate to come close to you.

The enemy pushes hard to destabilize you but cannot because you are firmly stabilized on Christ the Solid Rock.

Shine for the more you make others better, the better you become.

You know that the only secret to perfect peace is to firmly allow your mind to stay on God.

You're not prideful, you just shine because your God fulfills His promises to you; He is just and faithful like that.

Feel good for kind people, like you, are special kind of people.

Hope in God transforms weakness to strength.

We're supposed to have one enemy; that's your belief and I know you're sticking to it.

Don't give up, continue to shine for your light is highly needed.

Unity in good works bothers the enemies of progress, so bother them.

Those who tell you, only, about your negatives are not God's messengers.

The devil is obsessed with you because you matter; ignore the nincompoop and focus on the matters that matter.

Persist with your style that promotes peace, love, unity, and improvement for you'll be rewarded again.

Do not be too quick to criticize.

Keep shinning and ignore the Judases for God allows these betrayals and challenges to prepare you because you cannot become a warrior without going through rough times or training.

Regardless of circumstances, continue to operate in love because love rules.

They treat you with respect because you treat them with respect.

Shine because the angels of peace, love, and prosperity are assigned to you.

You're different and humble, not timid, "For the spirit God installed in you does not make you timid, but gives you power, love and a sound mind."

Glow, rejoice, and persist with your good plan for God has instructed people in critical areas to help you.

A good attitude is your greatest asset, so continue to flaunt it boldly.

Repeatedly wear those garments of love, peace, and joy that Jesus provided to you free of charge.

Smile and celebrate the sufficiency God gave you and focus less on the temporary insufficiency that the devil reminds you of.

Huge harvests abound in the barns of the grateful hearts.

Feel stupendous today, not because everything is perfect, but because you still glow.

The resources for your sparkle come from above, so keep looking up not down.

There's a time to bridle your tongue and protect your dream, there will come a time your dream will make itself public.

Shine and don't stop doing good because of what someone said or did; soon you'll reap hugely, again, from the seeds gallantly sown.

You fear no evil, you're not dismayed at all, for you know in whom you believe and you're confident that He upholds you with His righteous hands.

Continue to be a blesser not a stressor.

Remain good to others, and others will remain good to you.

Praising you Father Lord ignites our fire; with songs inspired by you, we will not tire.

Fear not and keep shining for the God in your corner is greater than that rubbish.

Your God has the capacity to correct any thing that goes wrong.

God will continue to do great and new things in your life regardless of what the devil thinks.

The Solid Rock, the Good Shepherd, and the Lion of Judah is fully involved in your affairs from AM to PM, so shine.

Destroy that garment of bitterness that dims your glow.

Keep being yourself, for those who know you well usually like you a lot or love you.

Shine, for God has endowed you with wisdom to face today and tomorrow.

Continue to be nice to people without expecting something from them.

You glow

You know

In inexpensive outfit

You appear too legit

In expensive attire

Can't help but admire.

Notes

1. New King James Version – Holy Bible

Notes

Notes

Notes

Notes

ABOUT THE AUTHOR

Udo Fosby Ufomadu, PhD is an established publisher, government official, and author of several acclaimed books. He has served on boards, such as Safe Schools, a city school board, and a private school board. He is a church deacon and a chairman of a not-for-profit organization.

For copies of *SHINE* visit ucandp.com

It is also available at amazon.com

www.ingramcontent.com/pod-product-compliance
Lightning Source LLC
Chambersburg PA
CBHW081407070526
44583CB00020B/2710